THE BEGINNER'S GUIDE TO

crystals

THE BEGINNER'S GUIDE TO crystals

THE EVERYDAY MAGIC OF CRYSTAL HEALING, WITH 65+ STONES

LISA BUTTERWORTH

TEN SPEED PRESS
California | New York

CONTENTS

INTRODUCTION

The allure of crystals is a tale as old as time. These beautiful works of art were forged by the elements—they're pieces of earth that hold the knowledge and stories of millions of millennia. Crystals can be teachers, gentle guides, and sparkling sages that tune us in to our deepest truths and the energy of the world and people around us. Nurturing a relationship with the mineral kingdom can infuse your life with a sense of magic, one that expands and deepens as you further your journey with these captivating stones.

Harnessing the power of crystals is nothing new. Gems and minerals have been used as talismans and tools of emotional, spiritual, and physical healing since ancient times, by nearly every civilization on record: from the Greeks and Romans, who used them as medicine and protective charms, to the Mayans and Native Americans, who regarded them as a sacred connection to the divine. Crystals, and their high vibrations, are just as applicable to these modern times, if not more so. They give us a reason to be still, and ground ourselves in the earth's energies amidst the hustle and bustle of our everyday urban existence.

Working with crystals offers a healing way to clear blockages, increase energy flow, and balance your system. Whether you are familiar with crystal work, or have yet to interact with the energy of a stone, this book describes methods for using, creating rituals around, and maintaining crystals. It also offers specific information about sixty-eight different types of minerals—organized by the chakras they're associated with—that have a wide range of emotional, spiritual, and physical benefits. In other words, there's something for everybody.

WHAT CRYSTALS ARE + HOW THEY WORK

Before the sun or the moon, before life on earth and even long before the earth itself, existed minerals—interstellar stardust that witnessed the profound and cosmic creation of our galaxy. There are more than four thousand known minerals on our planet today, and their very make-up has evolved along with life on earth; living organisms and crystals have been interacting, telling a story together for more than four billion years.

Though these terms are often used interchangeably, minerals, crystals, and rocks do have distinct differences.

 Mineral: An inorganic chemical compound.

 Crystal: A mineral with a geometric structure featuring micro and macroscopic faceted planes.

 Rock: A solid mass made up of multiple minerals.

Crystals are quite the draw on aesthetics alone, but what is it about these minerals that makes them so healing?

 Energy: Crystals, just like all matter, vibrate with energy. It's this energy that you feel when you hold a crystal or are in the presence of a mineral that speaks to you. It is earth energy in its purest form—the knowledge of billions of years of life is held within the geometry of their structure.

 Color: A crystal's vibrant hue can affect us beneficially by offering a form of color therapy, inspiring passion or calm.

 Intention: Crystal rituals encourage you to dedicate time and energy to your hopes, dreams, and desires. They act as guides, teachers, talismans, and reminders to connect, quiet the mind, and heal the heart.

Crystals are a wonderful addition to a holistic way of life, and can be a healing and supportive self-care practice. Taking the time to work with these minerals is the first step toward meaningful shifts in patterns of thought and behavior. Keeping your mind open to their lessons and influence will only further your relationship with these incredible beauties.

ACQUIRING CRYSTALS: HOW TO GROW A PERSONAL COLLECTION

Working with crystals is an intuitive process, and a very adaptable one as well. You don't need to wait until you've amassed an entire collection of minerals to reap their benefits. You can simply start with the one you feel called to and go from there.

Choosing: The world of crystals is quite expansive, and so are the properties of each stone. Every crystal has a myriad of benefits, and you might find yourself drawn to one stone for a completely different purpose than someone else using the same type of crystal. Trust your gut and experiment with an open mind. You'll likely find that the crystals you are drawn to change depending on your needs and desires. If you think you should work with a particular stone because of a specific issue you want to address or get support for, but find you don't feel a connection to it, you don't have to force it. Instead look for the stone that feels right to you.

Buying: If you're able, choose your crystals in person. Often you'll get a feeling about which crystal will serve you best. Crystal shops and metaphysical boutiques offer a wide selection. There are also traveling gem shows; check to see if and when there's one in your area. If you're not able to buy your crystal in person, there are plenty of online shops and sellers. Because crystals absorb the energy of their surroundings, buy them from a reputable company that sells authentic pieces. Even so, you will want to cleanse every new crystal you acquire (see page 14).

Forms: Crystals come in different forms that can affect their energy or the way you use them. Just as you would choose a crystal based on its benefits and your current needs, select the shape and form that you are most drawn to as well.

Raw: Raw, unpolished stones arrive in your hands straight from the earth. Some people believe these stones have a higher energy, but you'll want to find out for yourself.

Tumbled: A tumbled crystal is typically smaller, rounded, and polished, creating a smooth surface that reveals the stone's vibrant colors and intricate details. Tumbled stones are easier to place on the body and take on the go, whether you carry them in a pocket or purse.

Shaped: Differently shaped crystals can offer specific uses or properties above and beyond the crystal itself. Crystal points can draw negative energy off the body when pointed away from it. Double-terminated points are great for balance, and enhance energy flow in both directions. A pyramid shape is believed to amplify the crystal's properties. When a crystal is shaped like a sphere, it reminds the user of the wholeness of the universe and the infinite energy that radiates in all directions.

HOW TO USE CRYSTALS IN RITUALS

The ways in which you interact with your crystals and experience their benefits is very personal. You might prefer to meditate with rose quartz, keep green aventurine on an altar, and sleep with amethyst under your pillow. You might find that you prefer one method for a particular type of crystal, such as including it on an altar, and then find that you want to change it up by keeping it in your pocket. As with most elements of crystal work, let your intuition guide you.

CREATING CRYSTAL RITUALS

Creating rituals around crystal work can make the effects even more powerful and dynamic. Ritualizing also increases mindfulness, and is a wonderful self-care practice that promotes overall wellness. Here are seven ways to work with your crystals, along with suggestions for ritualizing.

Altar: Creating an altar gives your intentions and desires a physical form. It also gives your crystals a sacred space to work in.

Ritual: First, designate a space for your altar—a shelf or tabletop can work well. Smudge the area, burning dried herbs or wood so that the smoke cleanses the energy of the space. Choose your intention, pick the crystals and other sacred items that align with your altar's purpose, and arrange them intuitively. Create a new altar when your intention has manifested or when you feel called to hold space for something different.

Bath: Infusing bathwater with crystal energy by dropping water-safe stones into a bath is a gentle way to immerse yourself in their colors and vibrations. Drawing a warm bath is already a rejuvenating experience, adding crystals to this self-care practice will amplify its benefits.

Ritual: First, prepare the space where you'll be bathing. Perhaps this means dimming the lights, lighting candles or incense, or dabbing a few drops of a calming essential oil on your temples. Draw your bathwater and add a few crystals aligned with your intentions—amethyst or rose quartz are both great for this ritual. Before getting in, draw a few deep, cleansing breaths, close your eyes, and meditate on your intention. Get in and let the energized bathwater envelop your body.

Drink: Drinking crystal-infused water is another subtle way to absorb a crystal's energy. Simply drop a crystal in your glass of drinking water or in a jug that can be left overnight. Not all crystals are suitable for this practice! Some have trace amounts of toxicity and obviously water-soluble gems should not be used. Be sure to do your research before experimenting with this practice.

Ritual: Combining moonlight with crystal water makes an even more powerful elixir. On the full moon, fill a glass jug or container with drinking water. Drop a clear quartz into the container and place on a windowsill where it will be bathed in moonlight overnight. Drink the gentle, feminine energy of the moon paired with the purification of clear quartz.

Grid: Making a crystal grid—arranging stones to harness the power of sacred geometry—not only is a meditative practice, but can also increase the effectiveness of your crystal work on a particular intention. Grids can be as simple or intricate as you like.

Ritual: First, designate a space for your grid and clear the energy by smudging (see page 14). Set your intention, then choose the crystals that will support it. Decide which sacred geometry grid calls to you (find different patterns online that you can either print out or draw), and place your crystals in the pattern, starting from the outside and working your way in, keeping your intention in mind. Lastly, place the final "master" crystal in the center of your grid. Take a few centering breaths, and visualize your grid's intention.

Meditation: Holding a particular stone (or keeping it nearby) while meditating can enhance your practice, opening your consciousness and strengthening your connection to the earth.

Ritual: Choose the stone you want to work with (fluorite, celestite, and smoky quartz are good options). Find a quiet place to sit. Take a few deep, cleansing breaths; close your eyes and quiet your mind. Hold the stone you want to work with (or set it nearby), and imagine its energy permeating your body and soothing your mind. Focus on your breath as you hold space in this energy.

Physical contact: Placing stones directly on your body, especially over chakras (see pages 18–19), can help clear energy blocks and guide specific benefits to the areas that need the most healing.

Ritual: First decide which chakra you want to work on and pick a crystal that supports it. Lie on your back, take a few cleansing breaths, and quiet your mind. Take the crystal and place it on the chakra you want to cleanse, open, or heal—for instance, amazonite on your heart or iolite on your third eye. Visualize its energy radiating into your body. Continue for several minutes or until you feel called to stop. Take a deep cleansing breath and express gratitude, either internally or out loud, for the work that was done.

Sleep: Keeping crystals on your nightstand, or even under your pillow, is an easy way to benefit from their energies while you sleep. Calming stones like dumortierite are best for this practice.

Ritual: Just before you get into bed, dim your lights, hold your chosen crystal, and take a centering, cleansing breath. Visualize the crystal's energy, and the deep sleep you know it will give you. Place the stone in your pillowcase or under your pillow, and then drift easily to sleep.

CRYSTALS FOR EVERYDAY MAGIC

 HOME

These crystals are particularly suited for the home.

Crystal	Room	Function
Aragonite	Kitchen	Uses Earth's energy to enhance food preparation
Apophyllite	Guest Room	Creates a peaceful and calm atmosphere; allergy alleviation
Celestite	Bedroom	Brings in a positive energy; divine awareness; detoxification
Clear Quartz	Bathroom	Purifies and regulates energy
Pyrite	Entrance	Provides protection; grounding and uplifting
Selenite	Living Room	Clears negative energy to create a sacred space
Smoky Quartz	Office	Absorbs electromagnetic pollution

 WORK

Charge your workday with the positive energies of these stones.

Crystal	Function
Amazonite	Creates an environment for clear, confident communication
Black Tourmaline	Protects from negativity and electromagnetic pollution
Citrine	Encourages confidence, motivation, and creativity
Green Aventurine	Attracts abundance and enhances leadership
Sodalite	Promotes logic, order, and the sense of a common goal
Tiger's Eye	Provides stabilizing energy and attracts prosperity

TRAVEL

Once you've created a self-care routine that involves crystals, you won't want to leave home without one.

Crystal	Function
Desert Rose	Alleviates phobias (such as fear of flying) as well as motion sickness
Black Tourmaline	Repels negative energy; promotes physical, mental, and spiritual health
Hematite	Combats anxiety; grounding
Labradorite	Inspires adventure, protection, and a sense of magic
Malachite	Offers protection; boosts immunity and energy
Moonstone	Offers protection to travelers, especially through the night
Rhodonite	Balances emotion and nurtures love

 GIFTS

Choose a crystal with intention, and be sure to tell the receiver why you're giving them a particular stone.

Crystal	Function	Good for
Rose Quartz	Offers unconditional love; nurturing energy	Birthday, bridal shower, condolences, friendship
Amethyst	Helps develop inner peace and tranquility	Congratulations, expectant mother, friendship, get well
Herkimer Diamond	Encourages harmony and openness	Bridal shower, friendship, housewarming, wedding
Fluorite	Brings balance and protection	Birthday, housewarming, new job
Chrysocolla	Shares a feminine energy, tenderness	Expectant mother, get well

BASIC CRYSTAL MAINTENANCE: CLEANSING, CHARGING + STORING YOUR STONES

Working with crystals is not unlike nurturing a new relationship. They'll need some care and attention, and the more you give them the more connected you'll feel and the more magic you can expect to experience. Here are some general guidelines for maintaining your minerals.

CLEANSING & CHARGING

Just as crystals give off energy, they can also absorb it, which means cleansing and charging them is necessary. Cleanse any crystal that's new to you, unless it's been given to you with a specific intention as a gift. If you are using particular crystals to work through intense emotion or deflect electromagnetic waves, you'll want to reenergize them regularly. Use your intuition—your crystals will tell you when they need a boost. There are a number of ways to cleanse and charge your crystals. However, not all crystals are amenable to every process, depending on how porous they are.

Salt: Purifying crystals with salt is a common cleansing ritual and there are several ways to do it.

Method 1. Fill a bowl with water and mix in 1 tablespoon of sea salt per roughly 1 cup of water. Submerge your crystals in the water for 1 hour or up to a day. Rinse the crystal under running water and pat dry.
Method 2. Alternatively, fill a bowl with sea salt and bury your crystals (or place them on top of the salt) for 1 hour or up to several days. Brush off any remaining salt.

Smoke: Using the smoke of burning dried herbs or sacred wood to purify a crystal's energy—known as *smudging*—is a safe and efficient cleansing method. Sage and palo santo are most often used, but you can do this with whatever herb or wood you like. Using herbs that you've gathered and dried, or wood that you've felled and chopped imbues the ritual with more personal power.

To cleanse, carefully light a bundle of dried herbs or piece of wood, blow out the flame to draw a tendril of smoke, and move your crystal through the smoke until it has been fully enveloped.

Water: Water is another method of cleansing and charging, but make sure the crystal will not be adversely affected.

Method 1. Place your crystal in a glass or bowl and leave under running water for several minutes. Pat dry.
Method 2. Place your crystal in a mesh bag and submerge in a stream for several minutes. Pat dry.
Method 3. When it rains, set your crystals in a bowl outside for several minutes. You can also collect rainwater in a bowl and submerge your crystals indoors. Pat dry.

Moonlight: Harnessing the vibration of the moon is a powerful way to cleanse and charge your crystals. Its feminine energy is gentle enough that this method is universally safe.

To give your crystals a moonbath, at sunset, leave them outside or on a table or windowsill overnight where they will be fully bathed in lunar light. Full moons and new moons are especially effective for this method. Cleansing your crystals regularly according to the lunar calendar provides a simple and reliable reminder to partake in this ritual.

Sunlight: Imbuing your crystals with the masculine power of the sun is another option for cleansing and charging, but it is a method that's not appropriate for all crystals as some will fade and crack from the exposure. Be sure your crystal can withstand the light before using this method.

To give your crystals a sunbath, at dawn, leave them outside or on a table or windowsill where they will be fully bathed in light until sundown.

Earth: Recharging a crystal in soil is another nature-friendly method, especially for stones with grounding properties.

If you have a garden, dig a small hole and bury your crystal, marking it above ground for easy recovery. Leave overnight. If you don't have access to the outdoors, bury your crystal in a potted plant or herb container.

Visualization: Cleansing crystals with your own thought energy is another efficient and universally safe method.

Take a few deep, cleansing breaths. Hold your crystal in both hands and focus on the stone. Visualize a bright, white healing light forming at the center of the crystal and radiating out to encompass its entirety. Continue until you've visualized all the stored energy dissolving into the light.

STORING

Crystals are happy to be kept on display, especially if you are giving them regular love and attention and cleansing or charging them when the ritual is called for. But as your collection grows, or if you want to work with particular stones, you may want to store some crystals. First, separate tumbled stones from raw ones, and pay extra attention to particularly delicate crystals. Once you've grouped them, you can organize your stones however you like, such as by size, color, or chakra connection. Keeping them in cloth drawstring bags is the most space-efficient way to protect your crystals. Lined wooden trinket boxes are also useful. If you have extra drawer space, you can keep them there, using small boxes to separate them Use a silk scarf or other soft fabric to wrap any that need extra protection.

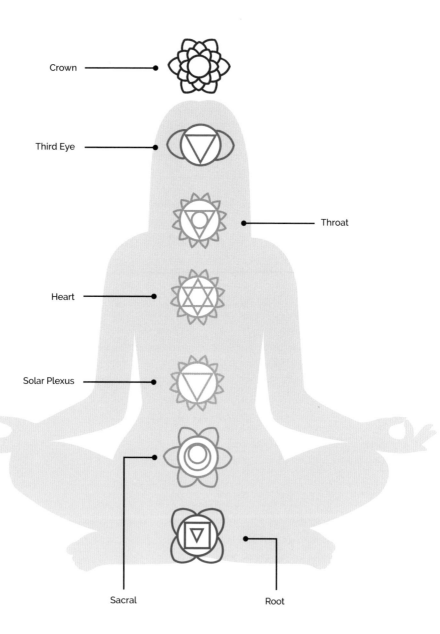

Crown

Third Eye

Throat

Heart

Solar Plexus

Sacral

Root

CHAKRAS + CRYSTALS: BALANCE YOUR ENERGY WITH MINERALS

Chakras are centers of spiritual energy that exist along the spine of the body, from your pelvic floor to the crown of your head. The word *chakra* comes from Sanskrit, meaning "wheel" or "circle," and the system was developed in India many millennia ago. Every crystal corresponds to one or more chakras, offering a gently healing way to clear blockages, increase energy flow, and balance your system. Here are the seven main chakras and a beneficial crystal for each.

Chakra	Crystal	Function
Crown: Spirituality and divine knowledge	Amethyst	Awakening spirituality
Third Eye: Intuition and wisdom	Dumortierite	Intuition
Throat: Communication and self-expression	Amazonite	Truth illumination
Heart: Love & compassion	Chrysocolla	Tenderness
Solar Plexus: Empowerment and self-respect	Sunstone	Energizing
Sacral: Pleasure and creativity; emotional center	Zincite	Passion
Root: Foundation; physical survival, including finances & food	Red Jasper	Vitality

In addition to these commonly known chakras, there are others that reside inside and outside of the body. Below the Root chakra are the Earth and Higher Earth chakras, above the Crown are the Higher Heart and Higher Crown chakras.

HEALING
CRYSTALS

A guide to working with crystals by chakra.

AMAZONITE

Tranquility + Clarity + Communication

 Color: Blue-Green

 Chakra: Throat + Heart

 Common Origins: Brazil, Russia, United States

Why It's Magic: Amazonite helps illuminate the truth. This semi-opaque stone promotes excellent communication, guiding you to speak clearly from the heart without being influenced by superfluous emotion or fear of confrontation. It's also incredibly soothing; it will dispel anxiety and neutralize negative thoughts and energy.

Amazonite brings good luck—it's a stone of manifestation, especially when you pair it with the power of the spoken word. It balances masculine and feminine energies as well as the various systems of the body, encouraging overall good health. It also protects you from electromagnetic pollution.

Notes: Amazonite is named for its hue's resemblance to the waters of the Amazon River. The blue-green color is caused by small quantities of lead and water.

USES

 Personal: Hold the stone while repeating a mantra you would like to manifest.

 Home: Set next to your computer to protect against the electromagnetic waves.

 Work: Enhances communication and your ability to speak with confidence.

AMBER

Happiness + Protection + Prosperity

 Color: Orange

 Chakra: Solar Plexus

 Common Origins: Baltic Sea Region, Mexico, United States

Why It's Magic: Amber brings a sunny disposition, transmuting negative energy into positivity. It offers warmth and comfort, increasing feelings of self-worth and gently drawing out your inner radiance—perhaps that's why it's also known to attract love. This ancient resin is soothing and protective. It can relieve anxiety and create an energetic shield, enhancing feelings of safety and security. Amber is often called a stone of courage, and will help inspire you to take the necessary steps to realizing your potential. It's a gentle healer, balancing and cleansing the systems of the body. It's also believed to have anti-inflammatory benefits.

Notes: Amber is fossilized tree sap and may contain organic material such as bugs or plant detritus. The oldest amber identified dates back 320 million years.

USES

 Personal: Wearing amber helps calm anxieties and attract romantic energy if you're looking for a partner.

 Home: Increases harmony and provides protection from external negative energy.

 Work: Fosters cooperation and congenial communication.

AMETHYST

Peace + Spirituality + Purifying

Color: Purple

Chakra: Crown + Third Eye

Common Origins: Brazil, Mexico, South Africa

Why It's Magic: Amethyst radiates pure peace and tranquility. This gentle but powerful stone opens the third eye and will awaken your inner spirituality. It clears and soothes the mind for meditation, allowing space to raise your consciousness. Amethyst is also known as the stone of sobriety, used in ancient times to abate the effects of drunkenness. It's helpful for dealing with and understanding the underlying reasons of addictive behavior, both substance-related and emotional. As a result, it aids self-control and curbs overindulgence. The healing benefits of amethyst extend to all general areas, ranging from insomnia to painful headaches and eyestrain.

Notes: The purple hues of this quartz are caused by exposure to radiation and impurities, such as iron. Amethyst's name comes from the Greek word *amethystos*, which means "not intoxicating."

USES

 Personal: Meditate with a piece of amethyst on your third eye to feel its healing energy and clear your upper chakras.

 Home: Dispels negativity and creates a peaceful atmosphere.

 Work: Protects your space from adverse energy, either from coworkers or the environment.

APATITE

Self-Expression + Motivation + Balance

 Color: Blue

 Chakra: Throat

 Common Origins: Brazil, Russia, United States

Why It's Magic: Apatite facilitates direct communication and is a powerful motivator. This blue mineral is a catalyst for releasing the past; it can provide a greater perspective, helping you to appreciate the present moment. If worked with regularly, it can lead to a higher consciousness and nurtures the desire to be of service to the earth and to others, leading some to call it the "humanitarian stone." Apatite is known to enhance intellect and increase energy. It's also believed to be extremely helpful in easing food-related issues, supporting overall well-being by establishing healthy eating habits. Healers use it to support the skeletal system, believing it fortifies bones and cartilage and can ease arthritis.

Notes: Apatite is often mistaken for other minerals, befitting of its etymological origin, the Greek word *apate*, which means "deceit." Its blue hue is caused by the occurrence of manganese.

USES

 Personal: Place apatite on your throat chakra to clear energy and enhance communication.

 Home: Helps imbue a space with uplifting and positive energy.

 Work: Keep on hand to regulate energy flow and prevent burnout.

APOPHYLLITE

Illumination + Alignment + Self-Awareness

 Color: White

 Chakra: Crown

 Common Origins: Germany, India, United States

Why It's Magic: Apophyllite will help you truly see yourself. The peaceful and illuminating energy of this stone enhances mental clarity while also keeping your spirit grounded. It will grant you a deep self-awareness, helping you to understand the reasons driving your behavior and bringing them into balance for emotional and spiritual harmony. It relieves stress and will remind you that you're part of a much larger picture and greater collective energy. It aligns the mind and spirit, so you can make choices attuned to a higher vibration. This crystal's calming energy inspires deep relaxation and optimism. It's believed to support the respiratory system and help allergies.

Notes: Apophyllite actually refers to three separate but similar minerals. Its name is derived from the Greek word *apophylliso*, which means to "leaf off," referring to the mineral's flakiness.

USES

 Personal: Meditate with apophyllite to gain insight into negative patterns and how to change them.

 Home: Creates a peaceful environment with spiritual energy.

 Work: Promotes organization and efficiency.

AQUA AURA QUARTZ

Cleansing + Calming + Communication

 Color: Blue

 Chakra: Crown + Third Eye + Throat

Common Origins: United States

Why It's Magic: Aqua aura quartz is a life coach in crystal form. Though it is not a naturally forming crystal (see Notes, below), bonding quartz with gold gives the mineral a higher intensity, so it can illuminate your path and give you the confidence to follow it. Aqua aura quartz also attracts abundance, though not necessarily in material form, reminding you of the more organic ways success can be measured. It's associated with the throat chakra, enhancing clear and heartfelt communication. This mineral also supports the higher chakras, opening spiritual pathways of communication and offering powerful psychic protection. This vibrational crystal increases energy flow and supports overall well-being.

Notes: Aura crystals are created by bonding precious metals to the surface of a crystal, drawing on alchemy to increase its power. To make aqua aura, gold atoms are fused to quartz, giving it a metallic sheen.

USES

 Personal: Meditate with aqua aura quartz to tune in to your life's true path.

 Home: Fosters positive communication and a prosperous environment.

 Work: Inspires ideas and helps direct your career trajectory.

AQUAMARINE

Courage + Calm + Fluidity

 Color: Blue

 Chakra: Throat + Higher Heart

 Common Origins: Brazil, India, Zambia

Why It's Magic: Aquamarine is a calming force in the storms of daily life. This gentle blue stone has a nurturing energy, and will inspire acceptance of yourself as well as external circumstances. Because it is associated with the throat chakra, it will help you speak from the heart without fear of retribution. It offers a rejuvenating tranquility and will cleanse old energies, instilling a sense of freshness and vitality.

Aquamarine provides closure, helping you to acknowledge the past and move forward. Its soothing essence allows for deep meditation, revealing inner knowledge and an openness to spiritual awareness. Pregnant women will find it particularly protective as it's believed to support a healthy pregnancy. Healers also believe it can alleviate a sore throat, ward off seasickness, and help with thyroid problems.

Notes: Aquamarine is a form of the mineral beryl; its blue hue is caused by the occurrence of iron oxide. Its name is derived from the Latin phrase *aqua marina*, which essentially means "sea water" and it was long used by sailors as a talisman while at sea.

USES

 Personal: Use as a worry stone, calming fears and encouraging acceptance.

 Home: Brings a sense of tranquility to a space.

 Work: Helps to mitigate the effects of daily stresses.

ARAGONITE

Generosity + Centering + Conservancy

 Color: Orange + Brown

 Chakra: Sacral + Root

 Common Origins: Austria, Morocco, Spain

Why It's Magic: Aragonite nurtures a deep connection to the planet. This grounding stone is imbued with earth energy, inspiring an appreciation of nature and the desire to protect and aid the environment. If you get lost in the clouds or are detrimentally distracted by fantasies, it's a gentle reality revealer. Aragonite shows the truth in a situation or relationship and provides the insight and acceptance to deal with it. It can lift a mental fog and bring a situation into focus. Aragonite increases patience and helps center thoughts and emotions. It also boosts energy, both physical and emotional. Healers believe it calms the nervous system, abating restlessness, twitching, and spasms.

Notes: Aragonite is a calcium carbonate; sand inclusions can give it a brownish hue. It was first identified in Molina de Aragón, a small municipality in Spain for which it's named. Aragonite is a component of both coral and pearl, and is what gives abalone shell its iridescence.

USES

 Personal: Hold aragonite before meditating to draw grounding energy and settle in to your body.

 Home: Enhances awareness of the way daily life wears and tears on the earth, inspiring environmentally conscious efforts.

 Work: Especially stabilizing when you're spread too thin or are lacking sleep.

AZURITE

Understanding + Clearing + Higher Consciousness

  Color: Blue

 Chakra: Third Eye + Throat

 Common Origins: Mexico, Namibia, United States

Why It's Magic: Azurite opens the door to truth. This deep blue mineral has been called the "stone of heaven" because of its high vibration with the third eye chakra. It will clear emotional and energetic blocks to reveal an understanding of the divine, deepening intuition and increasing spiritual awareness. It will help you gain a new perspective, allowing you to relinquish limiting thought patterns and long-standing behavior that's no longer useful. Azurite is also excellent for aiding issues with communication, whether you're afraid of making yourself heard or prone to nervously talking too much. Healers believe azurite increases circulation and is also beneficial for brain health.

Notes: Azurite is a copper carbonate with intense blue (which inspires its name) caused by the weathering of other mineral deposits. It is closely related to malachite (page 98).

USES

 Personal: Meditate with azurite to reset your mental state and tune in to your truth.

 Home: Fosters an environment of open and honest communication with a partner, family member, or housemates.

 Work: Enhances focus and decision-making abilities.

BANDED AGATE

Protection + Healing + Balance

 Color: Many

 Chakra: Third Eye + Root

 Common Origins: Argentina, Brazil, Mexico

Why It's Magic: Banded agate brings harmony to the mind, body, and spirit. Its parallel lines bring balance to yin and yang energies. Agate has long been used as a stone of protection and will act as a shield against negativity. It also soothes inner angst, calms feelings of anger, and mollifies internal conflict by illuminating the truth. Agate attracts abundance, but its energy is slow and steady, bringing incremental prosperity and success. This earthy stone offers a deep and grounding connection, but also clears the third eye chakra, paving the way for a higher consciousness. Agate is known as a general healer, alerting the body to its ailments so it can balance its own systems.

Notes: Banded agate is called the "earth rainbow" because of its alternating bands and variety of colors. Agate is named for the Achates (now Dirillo) River in Italy, where it was discovered by the Greek philosopher Theophrastus.

USES

 Personal: Lie down and place agate on your third eye to clear mental chatter and gain a better understanding of the truth.

 Home: Promotes fidelity between romantic partners.

 Work: Enhances concentration and problem solving.

BLACK ONYX

Stability + Strength + Productivity

 Color: Black

 Chakra: Root + Earth + Higher Earth

 Common Origins: China, India

Why It's Magic: Black onyx is a stone of strength—emotional and physical. It enhances feelings of self-confidence and courage. It's also a stone of stability and is very grounding, especially during times of transition. If you feel the weight of old emotional wounds, black onyx will help you release the sadness and grief. In addition, it has the power to balance adverse energies.

Aggression and intensity are channeled toward a greater good, becoming motivation for achieving your goals. Black onyx increases self-discipline and willpower. This dark mineral is a powerful protector, and repels negativity. Healers believe it increases stamina, and can help replenish you physically after illness or exhaustion.

Notes: Black onyx is a form of chalcedony, a microcrystalline form of quartz. Sometimes, like agate, it is found with parallel bands of white.

USES

 Personal: If you're feeling reckless or out of control, work with black onyx to get centered and clear-headed.

 Home: Place in the home to protect a space, particularly after dark.

 Work: Enhances concentration and the ability to multitask.

BLACK TOURMALINE

Protection + Grounding + Purification

Color: Black

Chakra: Root + Earth + Higher Earth

Common Origins: Brazil, Namibia, Pakistan

Why It's Magic: Black tourmaline offers a powerful sense of protection. This grounding stone repels external negative energy and dispels internal negativity, creating a more positive state of being. It's a cleansing mineral, clearing energy blocks and aligning chakras to encourage the flow of energy. Black tourmaline's effect on the root chakra helps you connect to the earth, to your physical body, and to your spirituality, bringing a wonderful sense of balance. It can also be used to neutralize electromagnetic pollution when placed near a computer or mobile phone. Black tourmaline is believed to boost vitality, which in turn boosts the immune system.

Notes: Tourmaline refers to a family of minerals. Black tourmaline is more specifically known as *schorl* and derives its color from iron. Tourmaline carries an electric charge when it is heated or rubbed, which is why some call it the "electric stone."

USES

 Personal: If you're feeling overwhelmed or highly emotional, hold black tourmaline while meditating to feel energized and centered.

 Home: Protects a space from negative vibes.

 Work: Can neutralize antagonism with a colleague or superior.

BLOODSTONE

Purification + Protection + Courage

 Color: Dark Green + Red

 Chakra: Sacral + Root + Earth + Higher Earth

Common Origins: Brazil, India, Madagascar

Why It's Magic: Bloodstone is a great detoxifier—it purifies both physically and emotionally. Perhaps because of the mythology of its origin (see Notes below), it's also known as a stone of courage and sacrifice. If you're faced with a challenge, it can give you the determination and strength to face it. Bloodstone is deeply grounding but also has an element of mysticism.

It brings these two worlds together so that both your inner spiritual quest and the elements of your higher self can manifest in daily life. This stone also offers protection and can be wonderfully revitalizing if you're feeling mentally, emotionally, or physically exhausted. Healers believe it boosts immunity and is beneficial for any blood-related ailments.

Notes: The typical bloodstone, also known as *heliotrope*, is green chalcedony flecked with specks of red caused by iron oxide. Legend has it that bloodstone was formed at the crucifixion of Christ, when drops of his blood hit green jasper.

USES

 Personal: If you're feeling embattled, use bloodstone to recharge and access the wisdom you need to stand up for yourself.

 Home: Can protect, revitalize, and ground the energy of a space.

 Work: Its grounding and energizing properties make it a great stone for sustaining creativity.

BLUE AVENTURINE

Motivation + Awareness + Strength

 Color: Blue

 Chakra: Third Eye + Throat

 Common Origins: India

Why It's Magic: Blue aventurine helps you take charge of your destiny. This strong, calming stone can inspire you to cut ties with the past, let go of unnecessary energy, and move on—especially when it comes to bad habits or addictive behavior. It provides mental clarity, which helps with decision-making, and then offers the support and perseverance to move ahead with your goals. Blue aventurine has a steady, masculine energy, promoting deep reasoning and an inner peace. It can open you up to new opportunities and inspire adventure. It's great to carry for protection while traveling. Healers believe it can be used for pain relief and to increase stamina.

Notes: Aventurine is a form of quartz with reflective inclusions (often mica). The blue hue is caused by muscovite (a member of the mica family) or ilmenite (black iron titanium oxide) in the quartz.

USES

 Personal: If you're stuck in a rut, use blue aventurine to illuminate the causes and be empowered to change.

 Home: Creates a sense of calm and a steady flow of energy.

 Work: Can enhance confidence and leadership.

BLUE LACE AGATE

Communication + Peace + Tranquility

 Color: Light Blue + White

 Chakra: Throat

 Common Origins: Africa

Why It's Magic: Blue lace agate is a stone of expression. This lovely "lacy" chalcedony—a microcrystalline form of quartz—helps users find their voice and the right words to express their emotions without getting overwhelmed. Because of this, it's helpful in releasing old hurt and trauma, fostering the work it takes to name the pain in order to release it. It's great for all communication, enhancing mental clarity and confidence and instilling words with truth and power. This mineral can also alleviate fears of being judged, and is especially good if you have any sort of public speaking to do. Its peaceful vibrations create a sense of calm, allowing you to ride the waves of emotion without going under. Healers use blue lace agate to soothe red or irritated skin. It's also believed to relieve a sore throat and allay issues with the thyroid.

Notes: Blue lace agate get its name from its complex, lace-like look. The one-of-a-kind patterns are banded layers of chalcedony and quartz that form when a pocket exists in a host rock, filling in with microcrystals that change depending on mineral content.

USES

 Personal: Hold when reciting positive affirmations to increase their power.

 Home: Keeps the peace and can quell tension during confrontations.

 Work: Hold in your pocket or wear as jewelry when conducting a meeting or giving a presentation.

BORNITE

Joy + Creativity + Rebirth

 Color: Iridescent

 Chakra: All

 Common Origins: Austria, England, United States

Why It's Magic: Bornite is known as the "stone of happiness." Its metallic-iridescent sheen exudes a pervasive sense of optimism and reveals the joys in life, particularly in daily minutia or during periods of grief or sadness. It will not only help you recognize abundance, but will also give you a newfound appreciation for all that existence has to offer. Bornite is also a stone of rebirth, inspiring a fresh outlook, stimulating new perspectives and jump-starting creativity. Much like its many-colored exterior, this stone has the ability to clear and align every chakra, bringing the energetic body into balance. It's also believed to regulate metabolism, boost immunity, and enhance detoxification.

Notes: Bornite is named after an Austrian mineralogist, Ignaz von Born. It is a copper iron sulfide, and when its surface tarnishes it becomes iridescent. It is also known as *peacock ore.*

USES

 Personal: Place on the third eye to clear blockages and enhance energy throughout the chakras.

 Home: Clears a space of and protects against negative energy.

 Work: Particularly helpful when starting a new job or position.

CARNELIAN

Creativity + Courage + Confidence

 Color: Orange-Red

 Chakra: Sacral + Root

 Common Origins: Brazil, Germany, India

Why It's Magic: Carnelian is an energizing stone. It's a vibrant motivator, quashing doubts in order to pave a confident path forward. It's known as the "singer's stone" because it's said to make the user's voice clear and powerful. If you're a performer, carnelian will alleviate stage fright and help you come into your own on stage. It's great for anyone in the arts because of its creativity-boosting power. The mineral's fiery appearance translates to its emotional properties. Use it to balance the sacral chakra, which will increase passion and energy and strengthen your sense of identity and self-expression. Carnelian is associated with increased blood circulation, and can alleviate symptoms associated with premenstrual syndrome (PMS) and menopause.

Notes: The name *carnelian* is thought to be an alteration of *cornelian*, which has roots in *cornele*, referring to the Cornel cherry. Iron oxide impurities cause the hue of this mineral.

USES

 Personal: Carry when you need a confidence boost.

 Home: Keep in the bedroom to heighten romance and rekindle passion.

 Work: Abates indecision and procrastination to increase productivity.

CELESTITE

Spirituality + Intuition + Calm

 Color: Soft Blue

 Chakra: Higher Crown + Crown + Throat + Solar Plexus

 Common Origins: Madagascar

Why It's Magic: Celestite offers cosmic comfort, with vibrations that help open you to an expanded way of thinking. Like azurite, it is also known as a "stone of heaven," as many believe it aids communication with the divine. Celestite promotes a feeling of peace and well-being about your place within the grand scheme of the universe. Celestite can clear confusion, helping you to trust what is true and to work on your higher self—open your mind and your heart with this heady mineral. It can also enhance your dreams, fostering a pathway to the subconscious and the realms beyond the physical plane. It's believed to alleviate throat, mouth, and speech conditions and can help in detoxification.

Notes: The mineral takes its name from the Latin *caelestis*, which means "celestial." Pure celestite (strontium sulfate) is colorless, but traces of various impurities are thought to create its beloved blue hue.

USES

 Personal: Hold in your lap during meditation for heightened connection to the divine.

 Home: Put on your nightstand to promote dream recall and positive morning energy.

 Work: Alleviates work-related stress and anxiety.

CHAROITE

Generosity + Acceptance + Illumination

 Color: Purple + Gray + Black

 Chakra: Crown + Third Eye + Heart

Common Origins: Russia

Why It's Magic: Charoite marries spiritual energy with deep heart chakra love. This high-vibration stone has some powerful effects: it will remind you to be present in the here and now, while helping you accept the past and whatever the future may bring. It's a wonderful tool for enhancing empathy and inspiring the desire to be of service to others. Charoite can help you overcome fear and nurture the courage you need to get through a challenging or difficult time. It stimulates your body's energy flow and can inspire a great proliferation of positivity. It also opens a connection to the divine, creating space for spiritual guidance and insight. Healers believe it strengthens physical resilience as well.

Notes: Named for the Chara River in Siberia, near where it was first discovered in 1978. Charoite can sometimes exhibit chatoyancy, an optical illusion caused by a band of reflected light—also known as the *cat's eye effect*.

USES

 Personal: Keep near you as a reminder to live in the moment.

 Home: Helps make service to others a priority in a household.

 Work: Increases motivation and reduces procrastination.

CHRYSOCOLLA

Feminine Energy + Nurturing + Loving

 Color: Blue-Green

 Chakra: Throat + Heart

 Common Origins: Chile, Indonesia, United States

Why It's Magic: Chrysocolla offers a wonderful dose of tenderness. Its feminine energies promote sweet openheartedness and deeply felt communication. It calms feelings of anger and provides gentle but powerful support. It also increases your compassion for others, and will aid conversations with a friend, partner, or family member who is going through a difficult time. Chrysocolla will help you pass along loving attention and support. It's a soothing presence during times of stress or transition, and eases negative emotions and fear. Chrysocolla is believed to help all manner of health issues for women, from symptoms of PMS and menopause to the pain of labor and childbirth. It's also thought to balance blood sugar levels in both men and women.

Notes: The name is inspired by ancient Greece, where a chrysocolla-like substance was used to solder gold: *chrysos*, which means "gold," and *kolla*, which means "glue." Its bright turquoise color comes from copper oxidization.

USES

 Personal: Place on the heart chakra to replace destructive emotions with self-love.

 Home: Offers a gentle shield from overbearing or difficult neighbors.

 Work: Supports creativity and dispels stress.

CHRYSOPRASE

Joy + Abundance + Revitalization

 Color: Green

 Chakra: Heart + Sacral

 Common Origins: Australia, Germany, Tanzania

Why It's Magic: Chrysoprase is springtime in crystal form. After a long emotional winter, this revitalizing stone can usher in happiness and inspire true joy. It's also very opening, creating a safe space for the heart to give and receive love. For those new to crystals, it is a wonderful introduction, prepping your capacity for the healing energy of other stones. Chrysoprase can also enhance personal insight, stimulate personal growth, and attract abundance—while reminding you that you're worthy of it. It also inspires trust, in others and yourself; it promotes fidelity in both personal and professional relationships. Chrysoprase is a stone of forgiveness, softening grudges or regrets. Healers believe it stimulates the liver, enhancing detoxification.

Notes: Small inclusions of nickel give this chalcedony its green apple hue.

USES

 Personal: Place over the heart for a sweet, supported sense of openness.

 Home: Use to give your home an energetic spring cleaning.

 Work: Establishes a positive foundation at a new job or in a new position.

CITRINE

Abundance + Invigoration + Prosperity

 Color: Yellow + Orange

 Chakra: Crown + Solar Plexus

 Common Origins: Brazil

Why It's Magic: Citrine is a crystal of manifestation. It's known as the "merchant's stone" because of its ability to attract abundance, which has more to do with mind-set than money or traditional success. It teaches you to appreciate what you have, and find joy in all the riches life has to offer. It elevates confidence and self-esteem, so you can go after what you want.

It also has the power to move stale energy, making way for the heart's true desires. Citrine's vibrations will give you a positive outlook, making it easier to overcome setbacks and achieve your goals. It also gives creativity a wonderful boost. Citrine holds the power of the sun, which can help with fatigue as well as depression.

Notes: Citrine is a variety of quartz; its yellow tint is caused by iron oxidization. Its name comes from the Latin *citrina*, which means "yellow."

USES

 Personal: Hold during a visualization practice to help manifest your objective.

 Home: Increases the feelings of warmth and happiness in a space.

 Work: Enhances motivation and stimulates creativity.

CLEAR QUARTZ

Clarity + Purification + Restoration

 Color: Clear

 Chakra: Higher Crown + Crown

 Common Origins: Brazil, France, Spain, United States

Why It's Magic: Clear quartz can do it all. It's a great starter crystal because it is incredibly versatile and has wide-ranging benefits. This translucent mineral is full of light, transmuting negative energy and bathing you and its surroundings in positive energy. It is detoxifying—both physically and emotionally—and has the ability to clear any energy blockages and bring the body and mind to a balanced state. It's cleansing and energizing, creating an optimized foundation from which health can flourish. This all-around support stone is associated with the crown chakra; it will raise your consciousness and clear the path for higher awareness. It also amplifies the energy of other crystals it's around.

Notes: Quartz is one of the most common minerals in the world, and many other gems—amethyst, carnelian, citrine—are actually colored members of the quartz family. Herkimer diamond is a double-terminated clear quartz.

USES

 Personal: Keep a clear quartz cluster in your meditation space for a powerful boost to your practice.

 Home: Harmonizes and energizes an environment.

 Work: Boosts clear thinking and a positive outlook.

DESERT ROSE

Clarity + Cleansing + Protection

 Color: Light Brown + White

 Chakra: Third Eye + Root

 Common Origins: Australia, Mexico, United States

Why It's Magic: Desert rose gently dispels negative energy. Use it as a stone of protection to shield you from adverse influences. It also offers guidance in the spiritual realm, and helps you tap into your higher truth. If you suffer from anxiety or phobias, this peaceful mineral will help relieve them, and is an excellent chakra-clearer. Desert rose also has illuminating properties, revealing both the good and bad of any situation. It teaches us that life has both highs and lows—which is what makes it a meaningful existence. Desert rose nurtures feelings of appreciation and acceptance. Healers use it to relieve nausea and motion sickness, and it can help with gastrointestinal issues related to anxiety.

Notes: Desert rose needs an arid, desert environment to develop; clusters of barite or gypsum form around sand granules to create the rosette-like shapes that inspire this mineral's name.

USES

 Personal: Carry desert rose with you as a protective talisman.

 Home: Can help sustain a marriage or long-term relationship by bringing the bigger picture to the forefront.

 Work: Enhances decision-making and focus.

DUMORTIERITE

Patience + Lightness + Spirituality

 Color: Blue

 Chakra: Third Eye + Throat

 Common Origins: Austria, France, United States

Why It's Magic: Dumortierite has the power to calm. This soothing blue mineral can alleviate both anger and anxiety, creating a sense of well-being and ease. You may find yourself laughing more, shedding the heaviness of negative emotions or thought patterns. This stone will help you break ties to people or things that no longer serve you; it's especially beneficial if you have addictive, compulsive, or codependent tendencies. Dumortierite promotes organization, and acts as a grounding element in the midst of chaos. It's also good for clearing the throat chakra, boosting your confidence so you can speak your truth. Meditate with it to open your chakras and help you connect to the divine. It can also soothe headaches and stomachaches and can help with sleep problems.

Notes: Dumortierite was named by mineralogist M.F. Gonnard in 1881 for Eugène Dumortier, a French paleontologist. Often found as inclusions in quartz, its color is thought to be the result of titanium oxidization.

USES

 Personal: Place under your pillow at night for help with insomnia.

 Home: Brings calm to a chaotic household.

 Work: Increases focus and self-discipline.

FLUORITE

Balance + Purification + Protection

 Color: Clear

 Chakra: Third Eye + Heart

 Common Origins: China, Mexico, South Africa

Why It's Magic: Fluorite is a crystal powerhouse. This stabilizing stone diminishes chaos and quiets the mind. It brings balance to the user's inner being and broadens perspective, aiding in decision-making and clarifying the path ahead. It's a very cleansing mineral, and can help shed adverse patterns, ward off negativity, and renew energy. Fluorite is known for illuminating suppressed feelings so that you can gently examine and resolve them. Fluorite can be used to disperse electromagnetic waves, and balances the body much like it balances the mind. It's also known for stimulating the immune system and is believed to strengthen teeth and bones.

Notes: This calcium fluoride crystal is often translucent, but comes in many other colors as well, each with its own set of healing properties.

USES

 Personal: Keep in your meditation area to increase concentration.

 Home: Balances the energies of a space, creating a harmonious environment.

Work: Promotes focus, cooperation, and creativity.

GOLDEN TOPAZ

Recharge + Charisma + Manifestation

 Color: Yellow

 Chakra: Solar Plexus

 Common Origins: Brazil, Germany, Russia

Why It's Magic: Golden topaz rejuvenates and inspires. It enhances energy and is a stone of attraction—it will bring you beneficial relationships and opportunities, as long as your desires are for the higher good. But even as it brings good fortune—success, fame, or wealth—it will make sure you don't lose sight of your principles and ideals. It has a gentle energy, and promotes an openheartedness and generosity. Golden topaz inspires creativity and feelings of abundance. It is also believed to recharge the body, alleviating exhaustion and fatigue.

Notes: In ancient Egypt, golden topaz was believed to have the glow of Ra, the sun god—Egyptians used it for protection and safety.

USES

Personal: Meditate with golden topaz for a boost in optimism.

Home: Offers protection and brings a warm energy to an environment.

Work: Brings about prosperity at work while keeping others from begrudging your success.

GREEN AVENTURINE

Opportunity + Comfort + Abundance

 Color: Green

 Chakra: Higher Heart + Heart

 Common Origins: India

Why It's Magic: Green aventurine is a good-luck stone. It attracts opportunity and can skew the odds in your favor. Green aventurine will make you want to leave things to chance. It has major manifestation power, and can attract abundance, money, and success. Green aventurine is uplifting and energizing; it creates an overall sense of well-being. It shields your heart from negative energy and protects you from relationships—whether a partner, friend, or acquaintance—that take more than they give. This stone also fosters an appreciation of nature and has a loving connection to the earth. It is an all-around healing mineral, bringing all systems of the body into harmony. Healers also recommend it for assuaging nausea.

Notes: Aventurine is a form of quartz with reflective inclusions (often mica). The green hue is caused by fuchsite (a chromium-rich mica) in the quartz.

USES

 Personal: Place on the heart chakra to clear blocked energy and soothe emotional wounds.

 Home: Brings a feeling of cheerfulness to a space and enhances the energy of possibility.

 Work: Inspires self-confidence, enhances leadership, and attracts promotion.

GREEN CALCITE

Prosperity + Inspiration + Balance

 Color: Green

 Chakra: Higher Heart + Heart

 Common Origins: Mexico, United States

Why It's Magic: Green calcite brings about the future of your dreams. This gentle stone releases deeply buried emotions. It helps clarify your communication so you can articulate your desires and better understand how to work toward them. It is a stone of prosperity and abundance—it attracts success and richness in love. Its calming energy is wonderful for soothing stress. Green calcite is beneficial for mental health, bringing balance to the mind, body, and spirit. It's an emotional anti-inflammatory, cooling anger and other negative emotions. Healers believe it's also a physical anti-inflammatory, helping to reduce joint pain and arthritis as well as to support fertility.

Notes: Green calcite is incredibly absorbent and must be cleansed regularly. Its green hue comes from the inclusion of chlorite.

USES

 Personal: Use as a stone of manifestation, holding it as you visualize your future.

 Home: Placed in a garden, it promotes healthy growth and organic abundance.

 Work: Keep near your desk and hold during times of stress for a dose of radiant, calming energy.

GREEN FLUORITE

Encouragement + Harmony + Purifying

 Color: Green

 Chakra: Throat + Heart

 Common Origins: Namibia, South Africa, United States

Why It's Magic: Green fluorite is a gentle healer, subtly bringing the physical and emotional bodies into balance. It helps reset the mind, quiet mental chatter, and clear a cluttered consciousness. This stone is very effective at dispelling negative energy (and should be cleansed often). It emanates an energy of encouragement and support. Its strong connection with the heart chakra clears painful past emotions and radiates love, strengthening and guiding your intuition in matters of romance and relationships. Healers believe it supports the immune system and helps your body integrate the nutrients it needs.

Notes: Pure fluorite is clear, but it exists in nearly every hue and is known as the most colorful mineral due to various trace impurities. It is believed that yttrium might cause the green hue of this fluorite.

USES

 Personal: Use as a worry stone if you're feeling overwhelmed.

 Home: Can help harmonize a challenging relationship with a family member or housemate.

 Work: Supports focus in a chaotic work environment.

HEMATITE

Grounding + Centering + Stabilizing

   Color: Black + Silver + Reddish-Brown

Chakra: Solar Plexus + Root

Common Origins: Brazil, England, Italy

Why It's Magic: Hematite is one of the most powerful grounding stones. If you're feeling overwhelmed or irrationally anxious, it's the best stabilizer to work with. It absorbs negativity (so be sure to cleanse it regularly) and helps with self-control. Hematite is sometimes referred to as the "stress stone," for its ability to assuage worries, or the "lawyer's stone," since it's particularly helpful for those seeking justice and dealing with legal matters. Hematite's centering energies increase focus and mental clarity, and balance the chakras. It is believed to help with issues related to blood, such as calming high blood pressure, combating anemia, and easing excessive menstrual bleeding.

Notes: Hematite comes from the Greek word for "blood," *haima*, because of the reddish streaks found on some varieties. It is one of the most common minerals and has magnetic properties that are enhanced when the stone is heated.

USES

 Personal: Hold in your pocket for grounding energy when feeling overwhelmed.

 Home: Maintains a balanced household.

 Work: Have on hand when dealing with contracts or other legal matters.

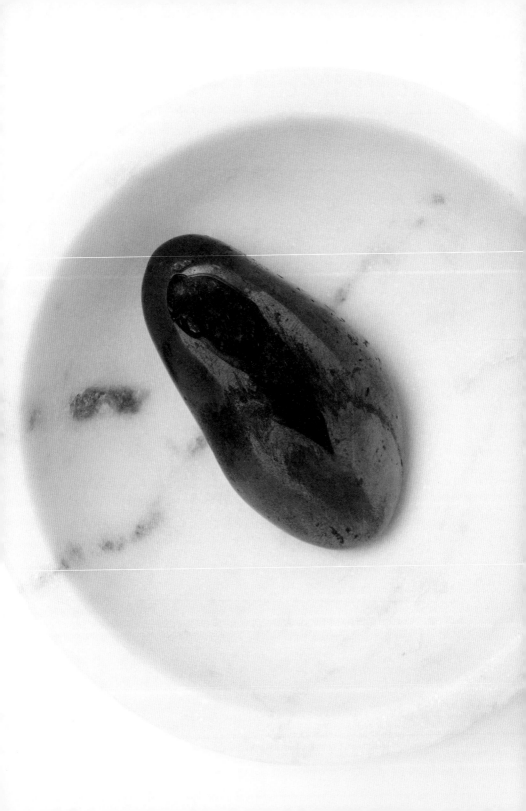

HERKIMER DIAMOND

Openness+ Amplification+ Attuning

 Color: Clear

 Chakra: Higher Crown + Crown + Third Eye

 Common Origins: United States

Why It's Magic: Herkimer diamond is a wonderful harmonizer. This clear mineral has a high spiritual vibration, opening the higher chakras and creating a path of understanding to the divine. It's a stone of attunement, able to gently put people on the same wavelength, or help you connect to a group or environment. It also acts as an energy cleanser, and has the power to store knowledge or emotion. Imbue it with love and healing and pass it on to a loved one. Herkimer diamond has the power to magnify the effect of other stones, so work with it in conjunction with additional crystals. Healers believe it can alleviate pain when placed in direct contact with the area that hurts. It is also known to relieve insomnia.

Notes: "Diamond" is just a moniker for this double-terminated quartz crystal, inspired by its clarity and diamond-like faceting. The name *Herkimer* stems from its discovery in Herkimer County, New York. Its origin dates back 500 million years.

USES

 Personal: Place on your third eye to open your chakra, allowing you to see and think more clearly.

 Home: If your household feels imbalanced or disrupted, a Herkimer diamond will evoke a sense of harmony.

 Work: Use to enhance your research capabilities.

HOWLITE

Calm + Self-Awareness + Openness

 Color: White

 Chakra: Crown + Root

 Common Origins: United States

Why It's Magic: Howlite offers a wonderful dichotomy: it attunes the mind to a higher consciousness while offering a subtle grounding. It stills the mental chatter of anxiety and stress, perfect preparation for meditation or a deep and restful sleep. Howlite stimulates inspiration and creativity, opening the mind to fresh ideas.

It tempers anger and calms fiery emotions. It will enhance your decency and integrity, which makes it particularly helpful for honest communication in difficult situations. If you procrastinate, use it to shift away from that behavior. Howlite is a stone that promotes preventative care, and is believed to strengthen bones and teeth.

Notes: This stone is named after the geologist Henry How, who discovered it in Nova Scotia.

USES

 Personal: If you wrestle with a short temper, keep a piece of howlite in your pocket.

 Home: Enhances an environment of openness and productivity.

 Work: Helpful when brainstorming, especially in group settings.

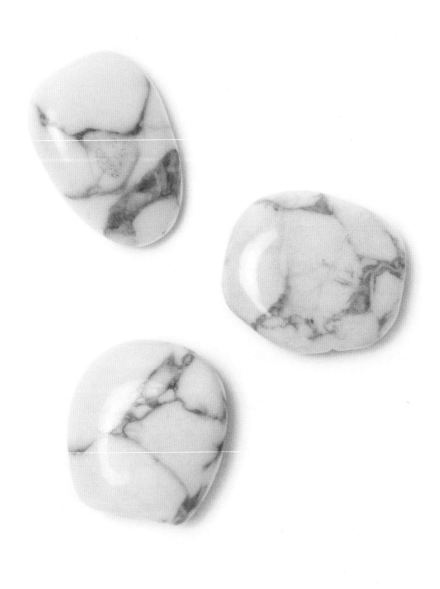

IOLITE

Intuition + Insight + Vision

 Color: Blue + Purple

 Chakra: Third Eye

 Common Origins: Brazil, India, Madagascar

Why It's Magic: Iolite is a truly visionary stone. Its tranquil colors act as a gentle guide to enhancing spiritual vision. It is also an emotional navigational tool, helping to raise your personal awareness and provide insight into addictive or self-destructive behaviors. Its energetic positivity will free you from past obstacles, negate disharmony with a friend or partner, and reconnect you to your true self. It stimulates creativity by opening new thought processes. Healers use it to detoxify the body and regulate metabolism.

Notes: Iolite has its roots in the Greek word for "violet," *ios*. The stone is pleochroic—it absorbs light differently depending on the angle, giving it the appearance of different colors. It is known as the "Viking stone" because Norse legend claims iolite was used to find the sun's placement in an overcast sky, helping with navigating the waters.

USES

 Personal: Place on your third eye during meditation to open yourself to spiritual discovery.

 Home: Display where it can catch the light and fill a room with happiness.

 Work: Inspires new ways of solving old problems.

JADE

Health + Prosperity + Harmony

 Color: Green

 Chakra: Heart

 Common Origins: Burma, Canada, Guatemala

Why It's Magic: Jade is a healing powerhouse. This beloved green stone can elevate all areas of your life, attracting abundance, supporting longevity, and bringing an overall balance and happiness. Sometimes referred to as the "stone of fidelity," it can heighten commitment, strengthen bonds between partners and family members, and increase trustworthiness. It can also act as a friendship magnet, drawing new relationships into your life.

Jade has also been used to increase sexual energy and reignite passion between lovers. In connection with the heart chakra, it promotes a general feeling of love and nurturing. It is also known as the "dream stone" because of its ability to facilitate the remembering of dreams and understanding their insight. Jade is believed to support overall health, but is particularly useful for supporting the renal system, as well as the spleen and liver.

Notes: Jade refers to two minerals, nephrite and jadeite. Its name has roots in the Spanish phrase *piedra de ijada*, or "loin stone," for its long purported benefits to ailments like kidney stones.

USES

 Personal: Place under your pillow at night to increase the lucidity and understanding of dreams.

 Home: Display jade to welcome abundance and luck.

 Work: Can help attract new business or opportunities.

LABRADORITE

Intuition + Creativity + Awakening

 Color: Gray + Iridescent

 Chakra: Higher Crown + Crown + Third Eye + Solar Plexus

 Common Origins: Australia, Canada, Finland

Why It's Magic: Labradorite is truly a stone of magic, used by healers, shamans, and psychics for its ability to enhance psychic gifts and raise spiritual consciousness. Turn this gray stone in your hand and a colorful iridescence will flash—it's a mineral that connects the realms of the seen and unseen, creating harmony between the physical and spiritual selves. It is also a stone of protection, creating an energetic barrier that deflects negativity and emotionally draining people. If you're feeling exhausted by the daily grind, labradorite will breathe new life into your existence, enhancing spontaneity, excitement, and adventure. It also sparks fresh ideas in the imagination, perfect for creative people stuck in a rut. Healers use labradorite to promote vision and also treat respiratory infections or cold symptoms.

Notes: Labradorite is named after Labrador—an Eastern province in Canada—where it was found by missionaries in 1770, though it was referenced before that in Inuit legends. The iridescent colors are caused by the reflection of light from submicroscopic planes in the mineral.

USES

 Personal: Use during meditation to enhance your introspective abilities, especially during a time of transition.

 Home: Infuses a feeling of newness into a stale environment.

 Work: Promotes cooperation and agreeability with coworkers.

LAPIS LAZULI

Truth + Confidence + Contentment

 Color: Deep Blue

 Chakra: Third Eye + Throat

 Common Origins: Afghanistan, Chile, Pakistan

Why It's Magic: Lapis lazuli is a stone of truth and knowledge. Its deep blue creates a peaceful atmosphere of acceptance—it will enhance your self-awareness and illuminate your deepest desires. If you have had difficulty in the past with being able to speak out, it will clear the stale energy of those experiences and make self-expression much easier. It will create the desire for information, inspiring quests for knowledge and even boosting memory. Lapis lazuli strengthens bonds with friends and family members, heightening a sense of loyalty. This stone is also great for working with dreams, and can be used to facilitate spiritual vision, creating a path for divine guidance. Healers use lapis lazuli to harmonize thyroid and other endocrine gland imbalances as well as to aid throat ailments.

Notes: Lazurite makes up the majority of this stone, giving it that intense blue hue; pyrite inclusions contribute to the glitter. *Lapis* is the Latin word for "stone" and *lazuli* is the evolution of the Persian word *lāzhward*, the name of the place where this mineral was found.

USES

 Personal: Place on your third eye to clear your chakra and stimulate spiritual awareness.

 Home: Inspires and nurtures loyalty with a live-in partner or spouse.

 Work: Supports integrity in the workplace and inspires trustworthiness.

LEPIDOLITE

Acceptance + Independence + Trust

 Color: White

 Chakra: Crown + Third Eye

 Common Origins: Brazil, Russia, United States

Why It's Magic: Lepidolite is a great mood stabilizer. It can bring balance to emotional swings and cool off fiery feelings. It's particularly supportive during times of transition—you might find yourself drawn to it when you're about to embark on a big change, whether you know it or not. It's also helpful in overcoming negative patterns and addictive behavior—substance-related and emotional—granting the ability to move on from the past and instill enough trust and love in yourself to go forward. It is a gentle but powerful stone, especially in the realms of self-respect and acceptance. Lepidolite's calming energy is also a stress reliever. Healers use the mineral for general pain relief, and it alleviates the physical symptoms of addiction withdrawal as well.

Notes: Lepidolite belongs to the mica group of minerals and contains a significant amount of lithium, though its rose and violet hues are more likely the result of manganese inclusions.

USES

 Personal: If you find yourself dwelling on the past, or are anxious about destructive patterns, meditate with lepidolite for peace and support to make the necessary changes.

 Home: Good if living in an urban area—it can create a sense of calm.

 Work: Promotes confidence in your capabilities, while attracting support from colleagues.

MALACHITE

Love + Harmony + Transformation

 Color: Green

  Chakra: Higher Heart + Heart

Common Origins: Africa, Australia, Brazil

Why It's Magic: Malachite is a stone that can inspire real change. It helps clear energetic blockages and inspires you to abandon old patterns, making way for positive transformation. It's a protective stone, absorbing electromagnetic pollution as well as negative energy, so be sure to cleanse it regularly. Malachite can open the heart chakra, making you receptive to unconditional love. It supports a healthy relationship, one rooted in love rather than codependency or need. The stone is also thought to be beneficial for travelers, especially those journeying by plane, as it can help abate any fears about flying. Malachite helps with energy flow, bringing the body's systems into balance and boosting immunity. It's better to work with polished pieces as raw malachite in large quantities can be toxic.

Notes: Malachite is a copper carbonate mineral, and gets its color from copper. It's thought that the name comes from the Greek word for "mallow," *malache*, a plant with green leaves of a very similar hue. Egyptians used its pigment as eye shadow!

USES

Personal: Use malachite for a visual meditation, focusing your mind on its entrancing bands and swirls.

Home: Display near a television to absorb electromagnetic pollution.

Work: Place near a computer to neutralize emission.

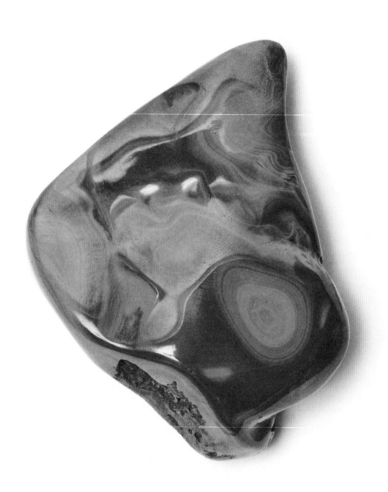

MANGANO CALCITE

Self-Love + Compassion + Feminine Energy

 Color: Pink

 Chakra: Crown + Heart

 Common Origins: Mexico, Romania, Slovak Republic

Why It's Magic: Mangano calcite has a sweet, healing energy. This is a stone of self-love and forgiveness. It will ease the pain of grief or emotional trauma, and restore your sense of self. This mineral distills fear, enhances confidence, and nurtures inner radiance. It has a wonderfully soothing effect on the heart chakra, softening sharp edges and raising compassion. It will teach you how to see the best in others and yourself. Mangano calcite can quell anxiety and prevent nightmares. It will inspire self-care, which enhances overall wellness. Its feminine energy is thought to promote the health of the female reproductive system.

Notes: Mangano calcite gets its pink hue from large amounts of manganese.

USES

 Personal: Meditate with mangano calcite when you need a dose of motherly love.

 Home: Creates a nurturing environment where love is freely given and received.

 Work: Helps you accept compliments and value the worth of your work.

MENALITE

Feminine Energy + Wisdom + Comfort

 Color: White + Cream + Gray

 Chakra: Sacral

 Common Origins: Canada, Morocco

Why It's Magic: Menalite vibrates with feminine energy. This calcium-rich substance is known as the "goddess stone" for its ability to connect the user to the feminine divine. It also has a very grounding energy, creating a deep connection to Mother Earth. Native Americans call menalite "fairy stones," and have long used them as good-luck tokens. This stone is particularly helpful during times of transition, especially for women. Menalite offers support in navigating the cycles of life and the changes that come with them, from adolescence to motherhood to menopause. It also helps with the physical symptoms of these transitions, easing hormonal imbalances. Healers use this stone for fertility and lactation support.

Notes: Menalite is what's called a *concretion*, a mixture of mineral cement that forms in the pockets of deposits left behind in lakes by glacier recession. Its name comes from Ménilmontant, a neighborhood in Paris, France, where it was first described.

USES

 Personal: For women, keep close when experiencing major life changes, for emotional and physical support.

 Home: Enhances a safe, nurturing space.

Work: Creates a sense of grounding in a chaotic or stressful environment.

MOOKAITE JASPER

Flexibility + Vitality + Protection

Color: Yellow + Brown + Red + Cream

Chakra: Solar Plexus + Sacral + Root

Common Origins: Australia

Why It's Magic: Mookaite jasper is like a motivational speaker in crystal form. This earthy rock enhances confidence, and helps you realize and work toward your full potential. It inspires the desire to try new things and break routine, while offering the support needed to positively navigate the unfamiliar. If you're stuck in a rut or have rigid ideas or patterns of behavior that no longer serve you, mookaite can help dispel them, promoting flexibility free from anxiety. It's a stone of strength and vitality. Mookaite jasper is also grounding and protective, creating an energetic shield that will make you feel safe and cared for. It's a very balancing stone, promoting overall health. Healers also believe it can strengthen the immune system.

Notes: "Mookaite" is the local nickname given to this specific opaline and chalcedonic radiolarite (rock that includes the mineral-rich remains of microscopic protozoa) that comes from Mooka Creek, in Australia. *Mooka,* an Aboriginal word, is said to mean "running waters."

USES

Personal: Keep mookaite in your pocket to assuage any fears when trying something outside of your comfort zone.

Home: Settles the environment after a move to a new home or during the upheaval of renovations.

Work: Reveals the root of procrastination and increases motivation.

MOONSTONE

Visionary + Accepting + Nurturing

Color: White + Beige

Chakra: Crown + Third Eye

Common Origins: India, Sri Lanka

Why It's Magic: Moonstone is the traveler's stone, providing protection as you travel, especially at night or by sea. It has immense influence on navigating change with ease and acceptance. Moonstone is helpful with big life transitions, allowing gentle space for personal growth, and also for more practical changes in one's daily routine, providing a sustaining touchstone for natural rhythms. Moonstone vibrates with feminine energy, softening the heart and allowing energy to flow. It heightens intuition and receptivity, helping you attain your highest self. It also promotes youthfulness—healers believe it can help slow the physical effects of aging. They also use it to support many female-related imbalances, including those associated with fertility, menstruation, menopause, and pregnancy.

Notes: Moonstone is a variety of orthoclase feldspar, composed of potassium aluminum silicate. It's marked by its adularescence, an optical occurrence caused by the reflection of light off of thin layers of alternating silicates that makes the mineral look like it's glowing (much like moonlight, hence its name).

USES

Personal: Wearing moonstone can enhance openness to spiritual guidance and deepen intuition.

Home: Helps ease the transition from the workday to nesting and home life.

Work: In a high-energy, ever-evolving environment, it can bring calm.

NUUMMITE

Grounding + Masculine Energy + Self-Discovery

 Color: Black + Iridescent

 Chakra: Third Eye + Root

 Common Origins: Greenland

Why It's Magic: Nuummite is a stone of self-discovery and empowerment. This ancient material facilitates a deep dive into your psyche, uncovering destructive patterns and hidden blockages, and revealing innermost truths whether you want to know them or not. It is a cleansing stone, sloughing away unnecessary baggage so that your true self emerges—this might be challenging, but it will inspire a sense of power and strength. It's also a very grounding stone, connected to the ancient depths of the earth. Many consider nuummite the magician's stone, as it is believed to enhance magical abilities. In addition, it provides psychic protection, warding off both negative energy and the effects of electromagnetic pollution. It energizes the body, and also allows for a deep and restful sleep. Healers believe it stimulates circulation.

Notes: Nuummite is perhaps the oldest mineral in existence, having been formed almost three billion years ago. It was discovered in Nuuk, Greenland. Its flecks of color are caused by the alternating layers within its fibrous structure.

USES

 Personal: Meditate with nuummite when you're ready to examine your past and move forward.

 Home: It brings a strong earth energy into an urban environment, reminding you to connect with nature.

 Work: Keep nearby for thinking fast on your feet and tapping into your intuition.

OBSIDIAN

Clarity + Protection + Self-Control

   Color: Black

Chakra: Root + Earth + Higher Earth

Common Origins: Argentina, Greece, New Zealand

Why It's Magic: Obsidian is a truth teller. It will expose your deepest being, release the past, and usher you toward a positive state of being. This stone can expose trauma and illuminate any falsehoods, supporting you in facing dark or challenging issues while reminding you of the light on the other side. Obsidian is a great protector, and can powerfully clear negative energy (be sure to cleanse it often). It will cut through mental chatter and indecision. This dark grounding stone also provides strength and self-control. Obsidian is believed to detoxify the body and aid digestion, as well as provide pain relief.

Notes: Obsidian is volcanic glass, formed when lava erupts to the surface of the earth and cools quickly.

USES

 Personal: Keep on your nightstand to alleviate stress and illuminate its underlying cause.

 Home: Use it to protect your space's positivity from being dimmed by negativity.

 Work: Good for protection in a hostile work environment.

PERIDOT

Protection **+** Peace **+** Prosperity

Color: Green

Chakra: Heart

Common Origins: Burma, Pakistan, United States

Why It's Magic: Peridot is a gentle catalyst for personal growth. It clears the baggage of destructive patterns, allowing you to let go of negative feelings and create the space for personal and emotional advancement. It is especially supportive during the natural cycles of life, easing the acceptance of transition. It promotes independence and helps you take responsibility for your own life. This heart-opening mineral also promotes fidelity. It emits strong vibrations of peace and offers a shield of protection. Peridot also dissipates hurt feelings, alleviating guilt and jealousy. It is a stone that attracts prosperity. Healers use it to treat imbalances in the endocrine system, which enhances the body's overall health and vitality.

Notes: Peridot is one of the few gems that takes shape in the earth's mantle, beneath the crust, formed in lava and carried to the earth's surface. Peridot's particular shade of green depends on how much iron it contains.

USES

Personal: Place on the heart chakra to release negative feelings about a relationship and increase joy.

Home: Creates a harmonious atmosphere, and enhances a relationship if you live with a partner.

Work: Eases stress and boosts prosperity.

PINK TOURMALINE

Loving + Soothing + Feminine Energy

 Color: Pink

 Chakra: Heart

 Common Origins: Brazil, Mozambique, Nigeria

Why It's Magic: Pink tourmaline vibrates with unconditional love. It is a gentle, nurturing, healing stone and offers emotional support in times of trial and transition. This mineral will open you up to all kinds of love—self, romantic, platonic, familial—and allows you to take pleasure in the process, relishing the vulnerability rather than fearing it. This tender stone heightens compassion and enhances empathy, for yourself and for others. It also attracts love and creates an atmosphere of peace and joy. Pink tourmaline soothes anxiety and helps ease depression.

Notes: Tourmaline refers to a family of minerals with a variety of hues and physical characteristics. Pink tourmaline's hue is caused by exposure to natural radiation.

USES

 Personal: Place over your heart chakra for a powerful dose of loving energy.

 Home: Creates an environment of compassionate communication.

 Work: Helpful when learning a new task or skill.

PREHNITE

Confidence + Calm + Realization

 Color: Green

 Chakra: Heart + Solar Plexus

 Common Origins: Australia, South Africa

Why It's Magic: Prehnite is a gentle but powerful self-esteem booster. If you're feeling a lack of self-worth, prehnite will enhance confidence, which amplifies your ability to speak your mind and say no when someone is asking too much of you. It's known as a stone of prophecy, instilling a sense of preparedness for and acceptance of what's to come. It's also a very calming stone, balancing energy and creating a sense of sanctuary. Prehnite is helpful in identifying the patterns and behaviors that have stalled your potential, and leaving behind what no longer serves you. This green stone also promotes a connection with and love for nature. Healers believe it can detoxify the digestive system and calm associated issues.

Notes: Prehnite is a rock formed by aluminum and calcium. It's named after Colonel Hendrik Von Prehn, the Dutch mineralogist who first described it in South Africa in 1788.

USES

 Personal: Hold prehnite while meditating to "see" your path of spiritual growth.

 Home: Use for spring cleaning—it will help with decluttering and inspire you to keep only what is useful.

 Work: Helps streamline a disorganized workspace and promotes good energy flow.

PYRITE

Masculine Energy + Empowerment + Protection

Color: Metallic

Chakra: Solar Plexus + Sacral

Common Origins: Peru, Spain, United States

Why It's Magic: Pyrite both protects and propels. It will shield you from negative energy and inspire you to understand what your full potential is and work toward reaching it. It clears the way for attracting success and prosperity and is also known for increasing willpower. Pyrite is an empowering mineral, enhancing yang (or masculine) energy, breeding confidence and revitalization.

It emits a general positivity and also has a deep grounding effect—it can draw chaotic or scatterbrained thoughts into focus and transmute apathy into drive. It has a very encouraging and uplifting energy. Healers believe its protective properties are also beneficial in fighting off colds, flus, and other contagious illnesses.

Notes: Pyrite has its roots in the Greek word *pry*, or "fire," because of its ability to create a spark when struck against stone or steel. It's also known as *fool's gold*, thanks to its metallic sheen.

USES

Personal: Hold a piece of pyrite at the end of a meditation to help ground the energy in your body.

Home: Helps center the energy in a chaotic household.

Work: Energizes a workspace and stimulates the creation of new ideas and solutions.

RAINBOW QUARTZ

Vibrancy + Optimism + Growth

 Color: Clear with rainbows

Chakra: All

 Common Origins: Brazil

Why It's Magic: Rainbow quartz is a stone of transformation. If you've experienced loss or are dealing with grief, this crystal can help lift you out of the darkness and encourage a renewed love of life, offering a fresh start. Just as it contains all the colors of the rainbow, it can also open and balance every chakra in the body.

Use it to support alignment both spiritually and physically; it's believed to energize and balance all the systems of the body. This mesmerizing quartz is also known to be a powerful manifestation mineral. It clears negative energy so you can focus on your true desires, raising your consciousness and bathing you in a loving light.

Notes: Internal fissures create the visual rainbows in this beautiful variety of clear quartz. It is also commonly referred to as "fire and ice" quartz.

USES

 Personal: Meditate with rainbow quartz on your solar plexus to clear your chakras.

Home: Place in a sun-filled room to enhance the crystal's positive vibrations.

Work: Use to help you cope with and rebound from a business disappointment.

RED JASPER

Passion + Insight + Stimulation

 Color: Red

 Chakra: Sacral + Root

 Common Origins: Germany, India, United States

Why It's Magic: Red jasper gently but effectively generates life force—it enhances vitality and replenishes depleted energy. It's also a stone of protection, warding off physical as well as mental threats. This grounding stone fosters a deep connection to the earth and radiates with stability in times of chaos. It is an excellent stone if you're creative because it will stimulate new ideas and can also spark renewed interest in ongoing works. Red jasper enhances endurance and vitality, and stokes the flames of sexual passion. Its stimulating energy will lift a mental fog, to remind you of the beauty and joy in life. Healers believe it aids circulation and that it is particularly beneficial for pregnant women, helping slow the loss of blood after childbirth.

Notes: Jasper is a combination of chalcedony and other minerals; its red color comes from iron inclusions. *Jasper* means "spotted stone," with etymological roots in Old French, Greek, and Latin. It is referred to as the "blood of Mother Earth" by some Native American tribes.

USES

 Personal: Sit with red jasper when you need to jump start your energy or creativity.

 Home: Keep this stone in the bedroom to rekindle passion or enhance sexual compatibility.

 Work: Enhances the ability to get things done while still promoting harmony.

RHODOCHROSITE

Compassion + Positivity + Love

 Color: Pink

 Chakra: Heart + Solar Plexus

 Common Origins: Argentina, Romania, United States

Why It's Magic: Rhodochrosite exhibits a powerful love. This pink stone is an emotional healing powerhouse, especially if you're feeling unloved or suffering from low self-esteem. If you've experienced childhood trauma or sexual abuse, rhodochrosite can help you face compartmentalized emotion, clear it, and open a path toward unadulterated happiness.

It also heals all manner of heartache—it tempers jealousy and enhances feelings of love and acceptance. Its energies are dynamic, inspiring self-love, playfulness, and an openness to vulnerability and intimacy with a romantic partner. This loving pink stone is a great teacher of the heart. Healers believe rhodochrosite can help relieve respiratory ailments, including asthma.

Notes: Rhodochrosite has its roots in the Greek word *rhodokhros,* meaning "rose-colored." This stone is a manganese mineral that in its pure form is actually red. The substitution of calcium for manganese in the crystal's structure creates its most common pink hue.

USES

 Personal: If you are feeling depleted in the area of love, keep rhodochrosite near.

 Home: Brings a sense of peace and positivity to your space.

 Work: Fosters friendship with coworkers and colleagues.

RHODONITE

Forgiveness + Compassion + Acceptance

 Color: Pink + Black

 Chakra: Heart

 Common Origins: Sweden, Russia

Why It's Magic: Rhodonite heals all matters of the heart. Known as both the "the stone of forgiveness" and the "rescue stone," it is perfect for both uplifting and grounding you after a relationship rift. Helps open your heart to the rosiness of unconditional love, while accepting that human relationships can also encompass pain. Rhodonite also provides excellent support during periods of great transition and personal evolution.

It's known to help uncover true passion, making the user feel more aligned with a purpose. It helps reveal toxic patterns of past relationships and encourages the acceptance to leave them behind. Rhodonite helps heal the inner self, so that you can spread love and service to the outer world. Rhodonite is also good for detoxifying the body and can enhance reinvigoration after the energy-draining toll of negative emotions.

Notes: In Greek, *rhodon* means "rose," inspiring the name of this crystal. Rhodonite is a manganese silicate; the black veins are caused by manganese oxidization.

USES

 Personal: Place over the heart chakra to release fear, mend heartache, and help break negative relationship patterns.

 Home: Enhances harmony or eases resentment between roommates or a live-in partner.

 Work: Helps to create a positive environment and improve your confidence.

ROSE QUARTZ

Love + Peace + Acceptance

 Color: Pink

 Chakra: Higher Heart + Heart

 Common Origins: Brazil, Madagascar, United States

Why It's Magic: Rose quartz is the love stone—divine love, self-love, romantic love, platonic love; it enhances all areas of the heart. This rosy crystal vibrates with tenderness and peace. Its nurturing energy instills a deep sense of self-acceptance. It can open you up to new love and romance, and also soothe the heartache of love lost. It strengthens the bonds of familial and platonic love, creating harmony and boosting relationships. Use it to find emotional balance in times of transition and to clear suppressed or wounded emotions, gently opening the heart. Rose quartz can also enhance sensuality. It is believed that rose quartz supports fertility, wards off nightmares, and soothes anxiety and tension.

Notes: The rosy to red color is thought to be caused by small amounts of titanium, iron, or manganese. In Greek mythology, the color comes from the blood of both Aphrodite and her lover Adonis after he was attacked by Ares and she got caught on a thorny briar bush in her rush to aid him.

USES

 Personal: Hold rose quartz while meditating to soothe emotional trauma and strengthen positive affirmations.

 Home: Keep on your nightstand to draw new love or deepen love and commitment with a partner.

 Work: Wards off negativity and creates an environment of peace.

SAPPHIRE

Wisdom + Spirituality + Calm

 Color: Blue

 Chakra: Third Eye + Throat

 Common Origins: Australia, Madagascar, Sri Lanka

Why It's Magic: Sapphire is the stone of wisdom, both earthly and spiritual. It is beneficial for dealing with problems of communication—it will help you understand yourself, better express your thoughts and opinions, and understand what others are trying to say as well. It also increases self-confidence, giving you the ability to stand strongly behind your opinion. Sapphire will encourage you to seek the truth and then reveal it. The stone's tranquil blue relieves tension and quiets an overactive mind. It also draws prosperity, by helping the user identify and fulfill their dreams. It's a stone that promotes unwavering integrity and a deep commitment or loyalty. Healers believe sapphire can alleviate insomnia and also promote better eyesight.

Notes: A sapphire is a corundum crystal, and though typically blue (caused by the inclusion of titanium and iron), it also occurs in pink, green, yellow, and other hues. In fact, a ruby is a red corundum crystal.

USES

Personal: Placed on the throat chakra, it can enhance self-expression and relieve frustrations about communication blocks.

Home: Promotes an environment of commitment and fidelity between romantic partners.

Work: Increases mental clarity and the capacity for wisdom.

SELENITE

Cleansing + Alignment + Clarity

 Color: White + Clear

 Chakra: Higher Crown + Crown + Third Eye + Solar Plexus

 Common Origins: Mexico, United States

Why It's Magic: Selenite clears, calms, and cleanses. This translucent mineral abates confusion, alleviates indecision, and opens up your ability to tap into your gut feelings. Selenite is connected to both the third eye and crown chakras, raising consciousness and boosting communication with the divine. Use it to clear the energy of a room and bring the emotional body into alignment.

It has a powerful, peaceful energy, which makes it great for meditation. Selenite also offers energetic protection and creates a safe, comfortable environment. The feminine energy of selenite is helpful for new mothers, supporting breast-feeding and bonding as well as fertility. Healers believe that it helps with epileptic seizures and insomnia.

Notes: Selenite is a transparent form of gypsum, a hydrous calcium sulfate mineral. With physical qualities that resemble the moon's glow, selenite's name comes from the Greek word for "moon," *selene*, which is also the name of the Greek lunar goddess.

USES

 Personal: Meditate with a piece of selenite on your third eye to clear the chakra and invite divine direction.

 Home: Brings balance and a feeling of sacred space to a room.

 Work: Clears mental clutter and enhances decision-making.

SERPENTINE

Awakening + Protection + Positivity

 Color: Yellow + Green + Brown + Black

 Chakra: Crown + Heart

 Common Origins: England, Italy, United States

Why It's Magic: Serpentine is a great guardian. It is both emotionally and physically protective. It offers a deep connection to the earth, and reminds you of the importance and beauty of nature. Serpentine helps clear the chakras, moving through energy blockages and giving the feeling of a fresh start. This mineral is gently grounding while it raises consciousness—a perfect balance, applicable to emotions and hormones as well. If you feel like life is leading you rather than the other way around, it will help return control to you. Many believe serpentine can awaken kundalini—the serpent energy coiled at the base of the spine—sending it through the chakras to the crown for the experience of enlightenment. Healers suggest using it to aid with detoxification of the body.

Notes: Serpentine refers to a group of related minerals—mainly antigorite and chrysotile—the color and texture of which resemble snakeskin. Chrysotile is considered serpentine but is a form of asbestos, and not to be used for healing.

USES

 Personal: Have serpentine nearby when you meditate to promote a deep, peaceful practice.

 Home: Protects your home as well as the people in it.

 Work: Use to protect yourself from gossip and badmouthing.

SMOKY QUARTZ

Anchoring **+** Pragmatism **+** Positivity

Color: Gray + Brown

Chakra: Solar Plexus + Root + Earth

Common Origins: Brazil, Madagascar

Why It's Magic: Smoky quartz is an antidepressant in crystal form. It alleviates anxiety and stress by creating a gentle calm. It transmutes negative energy, fostering an optimistic outlook. This earthy stone has a very centering effect, enhancing concentration during meditation. Smoky quartz can also be rejuvenating, giving the user an energy boost as it increases positivity. Use it to clear old emotional blockages to see what needs to be done in order to achieve your goals and desires. It absorbs the fear of failure so you can propel yourself forward, unabated. Healers use smoky quartz to calm the nervous system and relieve headaches. It also shields you from nightmares.

Notes: The gray hues of smoky quartz are caused by the activation of aluminum impurities, which change color due to natural radiation.

USES

Personal: If you're feeling overwhelmed or scatterbrained, hold smoky quartz while meditating for a deep grounding.

Home: Keep on a nightstand to alleviate daily stress and negativity as you sleep.

Work: Set next to your computer or your phone to absorb all the electromagnetic pollution.

SODALITE

Perception + Purifying + Awakening

 Color: Blue

 Chakra: Third Eye + Throat

 Common Origins: Afghanistan, Canada, United States

Why It's Magic: Sodalite is a stone of awakening. It offers a true sense of grounding while also opening the third eye to insight from the divine. It inspires an honest and objective sense of self, allowing for personal growth and expansion. Sodalite also enhances a sense of order and practicality, promoting logic while clearing a path to enlightenment. This mineral is known as the "poet's stone" for its positive influence on the act of writing, inspiring creativity tempered with a balanced and truthful perspective. This deep blue mineral will cool fiery emotions and can reduce physical heating of the body, making it a favorite for treating fever.

Notes: Sodalite occurs in the crystallization of sodium-rich molten rock, which inspires its name.

USES

 Personal: Place sodalite on your third eye to clear the mind and raise your perception of self to a higher level.

 Home: Enhances the creative energy in a household.

 Work: Helpful when working with others, to create the sense of a common purpose.

SPIRIT QUARTZ

Harmony **+** Spirituality **+** Patience

 Color: Lavender + Purple

 Chakra: Crown

 Common Origins: South Africa

Why It's Magic: Spirit quartz offers an emotional uplift, magnified by its many points. It radiates a general sense of well-being, bathing you in its energy. It opens the crown chakra, connects you to a higher consciousness, and enhances the assimilation of divine wisdom. Spirit quartz increases patience and compassion and aligns all the chakras. This mineral is beneficial for groups, creating harmony and agreement. It's a highly spiritual stone that can be helpful for end-of-life support and facing terminal illness, offering guidance and comfort not only to the person dealing with the transition but also the ones who will experience the loss. In addition, it can boost physical energy, helping to revitalize the body.

Notes: The texture and sparkle of spirit quartz comes from small druzy crystals that grow on the prism faces of a pointed quartz shaft. It's also known as fairy, cactus, pineapple, or porcupine quartz.

USES

 Personal: Place under your pillow to enhance your dreams.

 Home: Creates a unified, harmonious family environment.

 Work: Provides insight into discord with coworkers, and helps balance group dynamics.

SUNSTONE

Warmth + Joy + Optimism

 Color: Orange

 Chakra: Solar Plexus + Sacral

 Common Origins: Norway, Siberia, United States

Why It's Magic: Sunstone is like holding a little piece of sunshine. This warm, energizing mineral is the antidepressant of crystals. It's particularly helpful in combating seasonal affective disorder (SAD), radiating the effects of the sun to ease emotional dreariness. Use sunstone to replace negativity with optimism, lift spirits, and generate feelings of generosity. It's also known as the "stone of personal power"—it will help you say no when necessary, and to cut ties to an overly possessive partner or energy-sucking friend. As it energizes the mind and spirit, it also energizes the body and can help alleviate muscle and joint pain.

Notes: In Norse legend, Vikings used sunstone to locate the position of the sun on an overcast day, or even before sunrise or after sunset. Hematite inclusions give this feldspar its sparkle.

USES

 Personal: Place on the solar plexus for an emotional pick-me-up.

 Home: Keep in the house during winter, to create a sunny atmosphere indoors.

 Work: Inspires leadership and a positive environment.

TIGER'S EYE

Protection + Prosperity + Balance

 Color: Brown + Gold

 Chakra: Solar Plexus + Sacral + Root

 Common Origins: South Africa, Thailand

Why It's Magic: Tiger's eye brings a healing equilibrium. This stone carries both the energy of the sun (its golden hue) and the earth (its rich brown color), combining masculine and feminine energies and creating a balancing effect. It will energize you when you're exhausted and calm you when you're overexcited. It stabilizes emotions and is also quite grounding. In ancient times, it was used to protect against "the evil eye," and it still provides a shield deflecting negative energy or physical or emotional attack. It is also a stone of good luck, and will attract prosperity. It's helpful when working with money or making financial decisions. Tiger's eye supports a balanced effect on the body's systems, optimizing health and well-being.

Notes: Tiger's eye is created when quartz forms over crocidolite, dissolving the fibrous mineral and creating the layered *cat's eye effect*. Its brown color is caused by the iron oxides and hydroxides of the crocidolite.

USES

Personal: Keep a piece of tiger's eye in your pocket to alleviate mood swings.

Home: Creates a balanced, centered household, particularly during times of transition.

Work: Attracts new business and helps in dealing with finances.

TOPAZ

Truth + Manifestation + Transition

 Color: Clear

 Chakra: Higher Crown + Crown

 Common Origins: Brazil, Nigeria, Sri Lanka

Why It's Magic: Topaz is a truth illuminator. This stone will help you discern fact from fiction and enhance mental clarity. It also brings great joy and abundance, known as a stone of good fortune. It will boost your energy and motivate you as well. It has a great manifesting power, creating a clear path to your goals and providing the emotional capacity necessary to go after them. Topaz also facilitates transition—it will bring about the positive changes that you're ready for. It helps the body regulate itself, balance energy, and maintain the most beneficial weight, as well as aiding with sleep and digestion.

Notes: Topaz gets its name from *Topázios*, the name of a Greek island where the mineral peridot was first discovered, which, until modern mineralogy, was often confused with topaz.

USES

 Personal: Hold in your palm while meditating on positive affirmations to increase manifestations.

 Home: Balances the emotional environment of a space and attracts abundance.

 Work: Enhances problem solving abilities.

TURQUOISE

Communication + Release + Healing

 Color: Blue-green

 Chakra: Throat

 Common Origins: Egypt, Iran, United States

Why It's Magic: Turquoise is known as a master healer. It soothes both the emotional and physical body, enhancing spiritual connection. It is a stone of communication, great for anyone who has trouble speaking their mind or has a fear of public speaking. Working with turquoise can help you cut ties to negative patterns of thought, supporting the release of guilt and regret from past actions and experiences. It supports a sense of optimism, letting you move forward emotionally unencumbered. Turquoise is also known for enhancing inner strength and leadership. The calming, wise energy of this mineral also balances masculine and feminine energies. Turquoise can provide a boost of energy to the exhausted. Healers use it for immune support and believe it detoxifies the body.

Notes: Turquoise mined in Persia was brought to Europe through Turkey, which is why its name is derived from the French word for "Turkish," *turquois*.

USES

 Personal: Place on the throat chakra to free your voice and speak your truth.

 Home: Supports clear and caring communication in a household.

 Work: Helps with self-expression and is especially good for artists and writers.

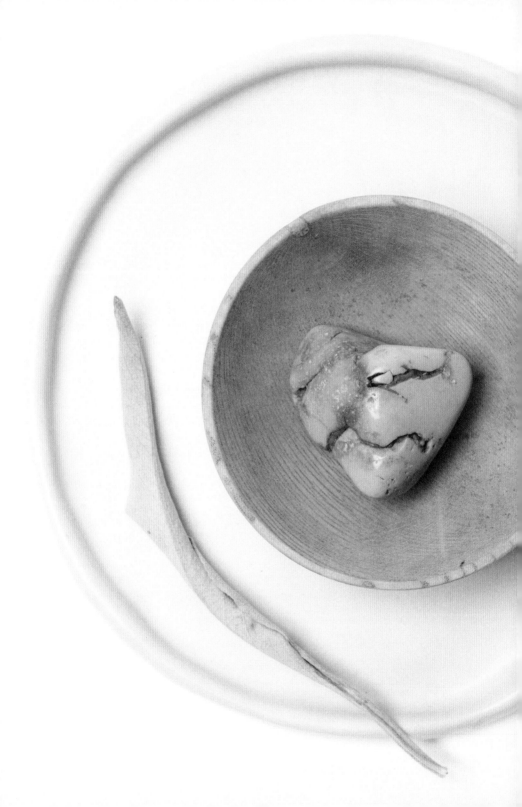

VARISCITE

Courage + Lightheartedness + Compassion

 Color: Green

 Chakra: Heart + Solar Plexus

 Common Origins: Australia, Germany, United States

Why It's Magic: Variscite is a peaceful, lighthearted stone. This light green mineral can soothe the mind and energize the body. It helps lift the mood of those who are very serious, alleviating heavy energy. It's especially useful for those who are uncomfortable in unfamiliar social situations, or have an aversion to networking—it mollifies the associated anxieties and helps foster an ease of connection. Variscite opens the heart chakra and infuses it with healing love and support. It also vibrates with the sacredness of nature, reminding you to appreciate and connect with the world's beauty. Healers believe it can calm and balance the nervous system.

Notes: Variscite is a hydrated aluminum phosphate whose green hue is caused by inclusions of chromium. The mineral is named after Variscia, what is now Vogtland in Germany, where it was first described.

USES

 Personal: Meditate with variscite to quiet mental chatter and ground yourself with its earth energy.

 Home: Can help find common ground and connection with a new or difficult housemate.

  Work: Use as a worry stone to calm nervousness about a particular project or presentation.

YELLOW CALCITE

Confidence + Optimism + Clearing

 Color: Yellow

 Chakra: Solar Plexus + Sacral

 Common Origins: Brazil, Peru

Why It's Magic: Yellow calcite has the dual ability to calm and energize. It can sweep negative energy out of a space and clear the mind of adverse chatter. Its gentle, sunny vibrations instill a sense of hope and optimism, transmuting anxious or sarcastic feelings. Yellow calcite gently clears old energy, awakening the mind and spirit to fresh ideas and ways of being.

This warm stone is also greatly beneficial when it comes to intellect—it helps increase efficiency, enhancing learning by boosting memory retention and the processing of information. Yellow calcite is wonderfully supportive for meditation, offering a strong calmness and openness to guidance from the divine. Healers believe this crystal can soothe the digestive system.

Notes: Calcite is a clear calcium carbonate, but comes in many different colors because of inclusions of impurities. Yellow calcite can range from translucent to opaque, from a light yellow tint to a more vibrant lemon color.

USES

 Personal: Keep yellow calcite in your pocket to boost or maintain a sunny outlook.

 Home: Clears negative energy from a room.

 Work: Helps balance priorities and maintain calm against deadlines.

YELLOW JASPER

Stability + Protection + Positivity

 Color: Yellow + Brown

 Chakra: Solar Plexus + Root

 Common Origins: Madagascar, United States

Why It's Magic: Yellow jasper is as grounding as it is uplifting. This mustard-colored stone builds you up, providing inner strength, resolve, and optimism during times of challenge. It deflects negativity and provides protection while traveling. It has a positive, nurturing energy that breeds hope and will inspire you to seek an optimistic perspective. It builds and attracts friendship, helping when fostering a community. Yellow jasper can also help you sort through complicated emotions, guiding you to an outcome that is truly beneficial. It also vibrates with strong earth energy, making it a very stabilizing, supportive stone. Healers believe it energizes the body, promoting general well-being, and alleviates nausea among other digestive issues.

Notes: The mustard hue of yellow jasper is caused by high percentages of iron.

USES

 Personal: Place yellow jasper over your root chakra for a supported sense of grounding.

 Home: Creates a nurturing atmosphere, especially during tumultuous times.

Work: Helps ease any rivalry between colleagues.

ZINCITE

Energy + Creativity + Manifestation

 Color: Yellow + Orange + Red

 Chakra: Sacral + Root

 Common Origins: United States

Why It's Magic: Zincite is the great stimulator. It will snap you out of lethargy, replenish your energy, and ignite passion—for life, a partner, or a project. It has a grounding power associated with the lower chakras, stimulating creativity and a sense of deep personal power. Zincite will enhance your intuition, clearing energy so you can tune in to your instincts. It's a powerful mineral of manifestation and can bring abundance and prosperity. Zincite is believed to stimulate metabolism and help with the body's absorption of nutrients. It is also good for healthy nails, hair, and skin.

Notes: Pure zincite (the mineral form of zinc oxide) is colorless. Its red-orange hue comes from manganese oxide impurities.

USES

 Personal: Use in conjunction with visualization to give extra power to manifestation.

 Home: Clears stagnant energy in an environment.

 Work: Dispels creative blocks.

INDEX

ACKNOWLEDGMENTS

Special thanks to Catie Ziller for letting me go crystal crazy, to Kathy Steer for making my words sound better than I do, and to Michelle Tilly for making it all look beautiful. Extra special thanks to Julia Stotz for her impeccable eye and photo magic. Thanks to Skye Whitley for the mineral management, to House of Intuition and Spellbound Sky for their gorgeous specimens, and to Caroline Hwang for showing me the Marabout ropes. Thanks to my parents, Pete and Jan Butterworth, my in-laws, Romualdo and Yolanda Avila, for the many hours of child care that allowed me to write, and to Ro for being the chillest baby around. Thanks also to my partner, Manuel, for always supporting my energetic endeavors and raising my frequency with his high vibes.

Library of Congress Cataloging-in-Publication Data
 Names: Butterworth, Lisa, 1977- author.
 Title: The beginner's guide to crystals : the everyday magic of crystal
  healing, with 65+ stones / Lisa Butterworth.
 Description: First American edition. | New York : Ten Speed Press, [2018] |
  "Originally published in French in France as A Beginner's Guide to
  Crystals: 65+ Stones for Everyday Magic by Lisa Butterworth with Marabout,
  a member of Hachette Livre, Paris, in 2018. Copyright © 2018 by Hachette
  Livre (Marabout)"—Title page verso. | Includes index.
 Identifiers: LCCN 2018039233
 Subjects: LCSH: Crystals—Therapeutic use. | Crystals—Health aspects. |
  BISAC: BODY, MIND & SPIRIT / Crystals. | BODY, MIND & SPIRIT / Healing /
  Energy (Chi Kung, Reiki, Polarity). | NATURE / Rocks & Minerals.
 Classification: LCC RZ415 .B88 2018 | DDC 615.8/22—dc23
 LC record available at https://lccn.loc.gov/2018039233

Trade Paperback ISBN: 978-1-9848-5654-8
ebook ISBN: 978-1-9848-5655-5

Printed in China

Design by Michelle Tilly
Photography by Julia Stotz

10 9 8

First American Edition